Not a Lot, Robot!

by Marie Powell

illustrated by Amy Cartwright

amicus
readers

Ideas for Parents and Teachers

Amicus Readers let children practice reading at early reading levels. Familiar words and concepts with close illustration-text matches support early readers.

Before Reading

- Discuss the cover illustration with the child. What does it tell him?
- Ask the child to predict what she will learn in the book.

Read the Book

- "Walk" through the book and look at the illustrations. Let the child ask questions.
- Point out the colored words. Ask the child what is the same about them (spelling, ending sound).
- Read the book to the child, or have the child read to you.

After Reading

- Use the word family list at the end of the book to review the text.
- Prompt the child to make connections. Ask: *What other words end with -ot?*

Amicus Readers are published by Amicus
P.O. Box 1329, Mankato, MN 56002
www.amicuspublishing.us

Library of Congress Cataloging-in-Publication Data
Powell, Marie, 1958-
  Not a lot, robot! / Marie Powell.
    pages cm. -- (Word families)
  K to Grade 3.
  Audience: Age 6
  ISBN 978-1-60753-582-9 (hardcover) --
  ISBN 978-1-60753-648-2 (pdf ebook)
1. Reading--Phonetic method. 2. Reading--Phonetic method.
3. Readers (Primary) I. Title.
LB1573.3.P695 2014
372.46'5--dc23
                                              2013044005

Illustrations by Amy Cartwright

Produced for Amicus by The Peterson Publishing Company and Red Line Editorial.

Editor Jenna Gleisner
Designer Craig Hinton
Printed in the United States of America
Mankato, MN
11/2015
P01286
10 9 8 7 6 5 4 3

This is my **robot**, **Dot**. She helps me with chores.

We have a lot to do today.
"Help me pick up my room,"
I tell Dot.

Dot picks up everything,
even my dog Spot.
"Wait," I say. "Not Spot!"

I tell **Dot** to make me a **hot** meal. **Dot** cooks **pot** after **pot** of **hot** soup.

"**Not** so much!" I tell my robot.

Next, I tell Dot to jot down spelling words.
But I don't want to study that many!
"Not a lot!" I say.

Then we take Spot for a trot. I am tired. But Dot keeps going.

"Dot!" I say. "Please stop."

At home, I lie on the cot.

"What's next?" asks Dot.

I say, "Not a lot, robot!"

15

Word Family: -ot

Word families are groups of words that rhyme and are spelled the same.

Here are the -ot words in this book:

cot	not
Dot	pot
hot	robot
jot	Spot
lot	trot

Can you spell any other words with -ot?